A SEASON IN GRANADA

Federico García Lorca

A SEASON IN GRANADA

Uncollected Poems & Prose

Edited and translated by
Christopher Maurer

ANVIL PRESS POETRY

First published in 1998
by Anvil Press Poetry Ltd
Neptune House, 70 Royal Hill, London SE10 8RF

This book is published with financial assistance from
The Arts Council of England

Designed and set in Monotype Fournier by Anvil
Printed in Great Britain at Redwood Books, Trowbridge

ISBN 0 85646 300 0 hardback
ISBN 0 85646 299 3 paperback

A catalogue record for this book
is available from the British Library

This translation is for
Patricia Findiesen (D/P)

ACKNOWLEDGMENTS

Some of the pieces in this book have previously appeared in Christopher Maurer's translations (since revised) in other editions of works by Federico García Lorca: "Holy Week in Granada" in *Deep Song and Other Prose* (New York: New Directions, 1980, and London: Marion Boyars, 1980); "How a City Sings from November to November" and the music for the two songs "El Café de Chinitas" and "Las tres hojas" (calligraphy by Carolyn Cassady) in *How a City Sings from November to November*, limited edition (San Francisco: Cadmus Editions, 1982). The publishers are grateful for permission to reprint them here.

A NOTE ON THE TEXT

All translations are by Christopher Maurer. All quotations from the letters of Federico García Lorca are from *Epistolario completo*, edited by Andrew A. Anderson and Christopher Maurer (Madrid: Cátedra, 1997). Sources for the Spanish texts of the individual poems, prose poems and essays are given in the notes.

CONTENTS

Preface   9

Poem of the Fair   13
Summer Hours   29
Palimpsests   37
Little Tales of the Wind   45
Water Jets   51
Meditations and Allegories of the Water   57
Daydreams of a River   60
Granada: Paradise Closed to Many   63
August...   71
Evening   72
Ballad of the Three Rivers   73
Tree, tree, / dry and green...   75
St. Michael (Granada)   77
Sleepwalking Ballad   80
Holy Week in Granada   85
Casida of One Wounded by Water   91
Casida of the Boughs   92
Ghazal of the Love which Hides from Sight   93
Ghazal of the Dead Child   94
Ghazal of the Morning Market Place   95
How a City Sings from November to November   97

Notes   116
Music: El Café de Chinitas   126
          Las tres hojas   128

Preface

In these pages the Spanish poet Federico García Lorca (1898–1936) celebrates the city in which he grew up and where he wrote some of his best work.

What we glimpse here is the ideal Granada – the "murmur of perfect beauty" – which quickened his poetic imagination and gave him insight into his own work.

García Lorca is an elegiac poet, who looks at what *is* and always thinks of what is *not*. His work sings not of love but of desire, and in desire there is more absence than presence. And thus the Granada presented here has little to do with the city around him, which he described, months before his death, as a "poor cowardly city, a miser's paradise, with the worst bourgeoisie in all of Spain." Looking beyond the here and now, shunning the "facile, abominable phenomenon known as the sketch of manners," begging "not for local, but for *spiritual* color," Lorca sought, and helped create, a Granada both eternal and universal. "From the local to the universal" was a phrase he often heard applied to the art of his friend and mentor Manuel de Falla. And his path to the universal was lyricism.

He thinks of his city, at serious moments, as a "murky palimpsest" where Christians commingle with Jews, Moors, Romans, Gypsies; where East blends with West in a drama that has made Andalusia into a true "island of culture." At more whimsical moments he imagines Granada as "a great legendary city: the perfectly realized poem that every true poet secretly hates." He evokes a time when "fresh garlands of roses and mulberries girded the city walls, and the cathedral, with its round rump, came forward like a centaur over rooftops of green glass; and at midnight, from eaves and balconies, oil lamps and cats in flight hissed at the perfection of the reflecting pools."

Custom did not blind him to the beauty before his eyes: the Sierra Nevada he could see from his window; the Alhambra ("jasmine of pain" in the moonlight); the verdant farmland of the Vega, with its clear, winding streams and cool poplar groves. Even the air seemed to possess a greater "spiritual density" than elsewhere. All this is caught here both in verse and in prose: in passages from his letters, in talks and lectures, in the early poetic sequences he called *Suites*, and in poems from three of his best lyrical works: *Songs*, *The Gypsy Ballads*, and *The Divan of the Tamarit*.

These writings, some of which are presented to English and American readers for the first time, give us a special insight both into Lorca's art and into the popular art which nourished it. Granada, he once remarked, "has given me her light and her themes and has opened for me the vein of her lyrical secrets… If God continues to help me, and if, some day, I win glory, half of that glory will belong to Granada, which shaped and molded the creature I am: a poet from birth, an incurable one."

It is an ironic truth that in 1936, in the first days of Spanish Civil War, Lorca was brutally executed near the city evoked so lovingly in these pages. "The crime was in Granada, *in his Granada!*" Antonio Machado exclaimed bitterly in a famous elegy. And yet Lorca's Granada lies outside history, beyond the reach of envy: a "perfectly realized poem," bright figure of desire.

CHRISTOPHER MAURER

A SEASON IN GRANADA

Every day I am more convinced of how marvelous this country is. If you were here with me, you'd be spinning like a top to see all four points of the compass at once. A few days ago, a green-purple moon appeared in the bluish mist of the Sierra Nevada, and just across the street a woman was singing a cradle song that tangled itself into the landscape like a golden streamer. Above all at sunset one lives in the totally fantastic, in a half-effaced dream. There are times when everything evaporates and we are left in a desert of pearly grey, rose, and dead silver. I cannot tell you how enormous this Vega is, and this little white village in its dark poplar groves. At night our flesh aches from so many stars, and we grow drunk on breeze and water. I doubt that in India there are nights so charged with fragrance and so delirious.

FROM A LETTER TO ADOLFO SALAZAR,
AUGUST 2, 1921

POEM OF THE FAIR

Under the sun of the tuba
the fair goes by,
sighing for old
captive Pegasuses.

The fair
is a wheel:
wheel of lights
against the sky.

The concentric circles
of the merry-go-round
ripple the air
up to the moon.

And there is a child
lost by all poets
and a music box
on the breeze.

Merry-Go-Round

Sad little horses
pierced
by lances of evil knights.

Down to earth you flee,
from a tale told backward,
from a field of old dragons
who have vanquished the saints.

Sad little horses
pierced
by lances of evil knights!

Fair in the Stars

The night open wide.

Spinning on the moon's axis,
God's carousel.

Far from the crowd
Sirius the poet
is sobbing.

Among the girl-stars
Ursa Major is dancing.

The cylinder of the breeze
spins over the treetops.

Dawn on the way,
and a little old star
sells snowy nougat.

The night open wide.

Fair in the Evening

When you go to the fair
in the evening
you enter a house of fireflies.

Rat-a-tat-tat
tat-tat.

You'll never see a ladybug,
they've flown away home.

Rat-a-tat-tat
tat-tat.

Madness of love,
what pain:
my heart feels delight,
exposed,
awaiting the arrow.

Rat-a-tat-tat
tat-tat.

Scream

Mosquito
moth,
bird,
and star.

What?

Star,
bird,
moth,
and mosquito.

On the ground,
my pierced heart
flies over the girls
of the fair.

Drum

Heart
of the fair.

Withered heart
beating
like a boy's.

No musician
has seen it.

It's the true
Pierrot, singing lyrically
to the moon,
which fits into
its ring
with a melody
of unknown love.

The drum glows
like parchment
(musical will o' the wisp)
and on summer nights
a thousand old moths
pursue its throbbing.
The drum is the nostalgia
of the road.
It sounds like the cloudy sky,
like infinite distance.

On the beached boat
of the circus,
on the country breeze,
listen to it throbbing!
Oh coffin
of the full moon!

Paper Roses

That man,
huge constellation,
Atlantis,
multicolor star
lost in the wounds
of flares.

That man,
with his cloud of laughter,
offers roses
to the winds
of childhood.

And that man,
the ghost of autumn,
saves roses
for dead children
and sends them
on a kite.

Moon at the Fair

At the fair
you don't see the moon.
There are too many moons
on the grass!

Everything plays at being a moon.
The fair itself,
a wounded moon
that fell upon the city.

Microscopic moons
dance in the glass,
and some of them pause
in the stormclouds
of the band.

At the fair
you don't see the moon
up in the blue.
You wait for it, sighing.
"My eyes are hurting!"

Dark Song

I'd love to lose myself
in your dark country,
María del Carmen.

Lose myself
in your deserted eyes
and play the keyboard
of your ineffable mouth.

In your endless embrace
the air would be dark,
the breeze would be downy
as your skin.

I would lose myself
in your trembling breasts,
in the black depths
of your soft body.

I would lose myself
in your dark country,
María del Carmen.

Swing Ride

The girl on the swing
heads north to south
and south to north.
In the parabola
a red star trembles,
beneath all the stars.

Confusion

Over the sleepless houses,
sonorous streamers.

Red   Yellow   Green!

The little square is flooded
with pipes and whistles.

Red   Yellow   Green!

The people go astray
in labyrinths of music.

Red   Yellow   Green!

The clock tells no hour,
the eyes have no looks.

Black   Black   Black!

Sunset of the Fair

Balconies close,
making cages for kisses.

So many stars,
so many of them!

A hurdy-gurdy
dies on the breeze.

More stars
and more of them!

But the poor Pegasuses
cannot close their eyes.

Just one star,
just one of them!

Variation

(Final trill)

Before the deserted fair
the poet is sighing

(wind beats on canvas).

His bird flies away,
over the frond.

Fairytale bird,
bird with no home,
singing its *pío pío*,
singing its *pío pa*.

27 July 1921
ASQUEROSA

Just now a great storm is beginning. The thunderbolts, like great black iron bars rolling down a slope of smooth stone, rattle the windowpanes in my house. Oh Lord, remember the flocks in the mountain and the wheat abandoned in the stubble! In the ashen light my mother, brother, and sisters say "Holy, holy holy!" Like a snail, I pull in my horns of poetry.

FROM A LETTER TO JOSÉ MARÍA CHACÓN Y CALVO,
JULY 1923

SUMMER HOURS

Knife grinder.
(Three o'clock.)
The soul of Pan
on the lips
of the knife-grinder.

What dusty
sadness!

He evokes
a green pool,
and something
in the branches.

He carries
St. Catherine's
wheel.

What sadness!

Five o'Clock

(Colt)

Down the deserted street
goes a black horse,
the wandering horse
of bad dreams.

The breeze of sunset
comes from far away.
A window is weeping
with the wind.

Nine o'Clock

Bloodless blue.
Velvet breeze.

Oh, my girl,
we can
go down to the well
of the heart,
down the river of words
to the island
of the kiss.
We can
sink into the thirsty
olive grove.

Six o'Clock

Birds push
on the evening,
their beaks carry off
the blue tail of day.

The sunset,
tattooed with weather vanes
holds up the boat
of the half moon.

In the cool fountain,
a serpent is singing.

Seven o'Clock

First star.
Everything looks toward Venus.
Like a girl
who has fallen down the well,
she shivers and trembles
as if to ask,
"Will I come back tomorrow?"

Eight o'Clock

Sky pulled off
its blindfold
and the thousand-eyed dragon
licks us with tongues
of wind.

Venus goes astray
in the crowd
and I remember a sweetheart
I never really had.

Thistledown at Night

In pulsing water
under the briars,
the stars are growing longer.

The light presses against my temples like a golden kerchief.
The trees dream of their fruit, the little leaves of their wind.
The cathedral bells are ringing and the airplanes are dancing
the rigadoon they do every evening. The Guardia Civil kills a
gypsy each day and writes down his name on a long undulating
list like a Chinese dragon.

FROM A LETTER TO BENJAMÍN PALENCIA,
JULY 1925

PALIMPSESTS

FOR JOSÉ MORENO VILLA

City

The ancient forest
pushes into the city,
but the forest
is in the sea.

There are arrows in the air,
and warriors lost
in the branches
of coral.

Over the new houses
a grove of holm oaks is stirring
and the sky
has enormous crystal curves.

Corridor

Down the high corridors
go two gentlemen.

    (New
    sky
    Blue
    sky!)

…two gentlemen
who once were two white monks.

    (Half
    sky.
    Mauve
    sky!)

…two gentlemen
who once were hunters.

    (Old
    sky.
    Gold
    sky!)

…two gentlemen
who once were…

    (Night.)

Air

Full of scars
it sleeps,
full of signs
and spirals.
Trail of the bird,
trail of a scream.

From the dust
of words and rhythms
two tones emerge:
black and yellow.

Madrigal

Oh, Lucy of Granada!
Dark little girl
who live at the foot of the Red
Towers... If your hands...
your hands...

   (Full moon.)

Oh girl of April!
Oh Melisendra!
You of the high towers
and spindle.
If your breasts... your breasts...

   (Half moon.)

Oh woman of my white
adolescence.
Fierce and fecund
Eve,
twisting in my arms
like the dry branches
of a holm oak
in the dance of the bonfire.

And my heart?
Was it wax?
Where is it?
And my hands?
And...

(Blind moon.)

First Page

TO ISABEL CLARA, MY GODCHILD

Clear fountain.
Clear sky.

Ah, how the birds
get bigger!

Clear sky.
Clear fountain.

And how the oranges
shine!

Fountain.
Sky.

Ah, how the wheat
is tender!

Sky.
Fountain.

Ah, how the wheat
is green!

In the rain Granada has that divine light from a pensive brow... light that reminds us of childhood. Light of six-thirty in the evening when we could come out of school and turn the corner.

FROM A LETTER TO MELCHOR FERNÁNDEZ ALMAGRO, 1927

LITTLE TALES
OF THE WIND

The wind was red
over the hill in flames,
and it has turned deep green
by the river.

Later it will be violet,
yellow and...
Over the sown fields
it will stretch out like a rainbow.

Pent-up wind.
The sun above.
Below,
the trembling algae
of the poplars.
My heart
is trembling too.

Pent-up wind
at five in the afternoon,
without birds.

The breeze
is wavy
like the hair
of certain girls,
like the little oceans
painted long ago
on wooden tablets.
The breeze
wells up like water
and spills
– tenuous white balsam –
on the sheep trails,
and faints
when it gets to the hardness
of the mountain.

School

TEACHER
Which maiden marries
the wind?

PUPIL
The maiden of all
desires.

TEACHER
What does the wind
give her?

PUPIL
Whirlwinds of gold
and maps superimposed.

TEACHER
Does he offer anything to him?

PUPIL
Her open heart.

TEACHER
Tell me what her name is.

PUPIL

Her name is a secret.

> (The window
> of the schoolroom
> has a curtain
> of stars.)

Granada looks splendid. Autumn has begun, with all the elegance and light sent by the Sierra. The first snow has already fallen. The yellows begin, deep and infinite, playing with twenty shades of blue. It is an astounding richness, which, no matter how stylized, cannot be captured. Granada isn't pictorial, even for an Impressionist. It isn't pictorial, just as a river is not architectonic. Everything runs, plays, and slips away. Poetry and Music. A city of fugues without a skeleton. Melancholy with vertebrae.

FROM A LETTER TO MELCHOR FERNÁNDEZ ALMAGRO,
OCTOBER 27, 1926

WATER JETS

Interior

From my room
I hear the water jet.
A finger of grapevine
and a ray of sun
point to the place
in my heart.
Clouds are moving
through the August air.
I dream I am not dreaming
inside the water jet.

Country

Water jets from dreams,
with no water
and no fountains!

You see them from the corner
of the eye,
never face to face.

Like all ideal things,
they are moving
on the very edge
of Death.

Aside

The blood of night
goes through the arteries
of the water jets.

Ah, what a marvelous
trembling!
I think
of open windows,
without pianos
and without maidens.

Garden

In the dark, four knights
with their water swords.
Four swords are wounding
the world of the roses,
and they will wound your heart.
Do not go down to the garden!

I am in Granada, and it's infernally hot... I've been working hard, and have "composed" some poems to the cuckoo (admirable, symbolic little bird) and the daydreams of a river, *pathetical poems which I feel deep within me, in the deepest part of my unhappy heart. You have no idea how I suffer to see myself portrayed in the poems. I imagine myself to be an immense violet-colored dragonfly over the backwaters of emotion ...*

*These days I feel pregnant, for I have "seen" an admirable book that has to be written, one which I would like to write: "Meditations and Allegories of the Water." What profound, living miracles one can tell about the water! The water-poem of my book has blossomed in my soul. I see a great poem about the water, part Oriental and part Christian-European: a poem that sings, in ample verses or (*molto rubato*) in prose, the passionate life and martyrdom of the water. A great Life of the Water with meticulous analysis of the concentric circle, the reflection, the drunken music (unblent with silence) of the currents. The river and the irrigation ditches have come deep inside me. Now one can truly say that the Guadalquivir or the Miño is born in Fuente Miña and empties out into Federico García Lorca, small-time dreamer and son of the water. I ask God to grant me strength and joy (yes joy!) so that I can write this book ... of devotion for those who travel through the desert ... I can already see the chapters and stanzas (there would be prose and verse), for example: The Looms of the Water, Map of the Water, The Ford of Sounds, Meditations on the Spring, Backwaters. And later, when I study (yes, study!) (pray to the saints to give me joy!) the dead water, I will write an incredibly moving poem about* the Alhambra, seen as the water's pantheon. I believe that if I were really to tackle this I could do something fine, and if I were a great poet, really a great poet, perhaps this would be my masterpiece . . .

From a little poem (Daydreams of the River), a stone in the portico of what I'm thinking about:

Slow Current

> My eyes go down the river,
> down the river.
>
> My love goes down the river,
> down the river.
>
> (My heart is counting
> the hours it is asleep.)
>
> The river brings dry leaves,
> the river.
>
> It is clear and deep,
> the river.
>
> (My heart is asking
> if it can change place.)

FROM A LETTER TO MELCHOR FERNÁNDEZ ALMAGRO,
JULY / AUGUST 1922

Meditations and Allegories of the Water

For many years now, as a happy boy and modest dreamer, I have spent the summer on the cool bank of a river. In the afternoon, when the admirable bee-eaters feel the wind coming and break into song, and the cicada is in a frenzy rubbing together its two little plates of gold, I sit down near the living depths of the pool and allow my poor frightened eyes to settle on the water or on the round tops of the poplars.

Under the weeping willows, near the tongue of the water, I feel the open afternoon gently settle its weight on the green surface of the pool, and gusts of silence cool the astonished crystal of my eyes.

At first I was moved by the splendid sight of the reflections, the fallen groves of poplar, which twist like Baroque columns at the least little sigh of the water, the briars and reeds which curl like the habit of a nun.

I saw that my soul was turning into a prism; that it was filling with immense perspectives and trembling phantoms. One afternoon, as I stared at the moving green, I noticed a strange curved bird of gold riding the ripples of a reflected poplar. I looked at the real poplar, which was flooded with setting sun, but saw that only the invisible little birds of the wind were playing in its leaves. The bird of gold was gone.

A marvelous coolness came over my whole body, tangled in the last little strands of sunset, and a broad avenue of light traversed my heart. Can this be possible?

Does my soul really journey to these waves and ripples rather than visit the stars?

The tinkling of sheep-bells placed a dark echo on my throat, and clear, tiny droplets spattered the marvelous skin of my soul. Ah soul, have you forgotten shivering Venus and the violin of the winds? Why do you hold to the resonant algae of the cascades, the huge bloom of the concentric circle? And I saw all of my memories reflected in the water!

Border

I was returning from the dry lands. Down below was the Vega, swathed in shimmering blue. The pulsing ribbons of the crickets were floating in the night summer air, which lay flat as a corpse.

The music of the dry lands has a markedly yellow taste.

I now understand that the cicadas are made of real gold, and that a song can turn to ash in the olive groves.

The dead who live in these cemeteries, so far from others, must turn yellow like the trees in November.

Near the Vega we seem to enter a green fishbowl, and the air becomes a sea of blue waves, a sea made for the moon, where countless frogs play their flutes of dry cane.

Coming down from the dry lands to the Vega, one must cross a mysterious ford which few people can feel, the Ford of Sounds. This is a natural border where a strange silence tries to deaden two contrary musics. If we had a well-constituted spiritual retina we would see how a man tinged gold by the dry lands turns green on entering the Vega, after disappearing into the murky musical current of the border.

For a moment I have tried to follow that wonderful dividing line (frogs on one side and crickets on the other), and where those two sounds collide almost imperceptibly, I have drunk fresh, cold little trickles of silence.

Who can go down this long road without his soul being covered with a confusing arabesque? Who would dare to say, "I have walked a road in my head; a road belonging not to fish or fowl or man but only to the ears?"

Is this the road that goes to No Man's Land, the land of those who have died waiting? From the tail of the olive grove to the first poplars, what admirable algae, what invisible little lights must be floating by!

I have drawn up before the current and the long antennae of my hearing have explored its depths. Here it is wide and full of whirlpools, but in the mountains it will be buried under blue sands of silence. Here it has the sublime confusion of a dream we cannot remember.

The waning moon, like a golden clove of garlic, gives the fuzz of an adolescent to the curve of the sky.

Daydreams of the River

The poplar groves are gone,
but they leave their reflection.

    (Ah, what a lovely
    moment!)

The poplar groves are gone,
but they leave us the wind.

The long sky has placed
a shroud on the wind.

    (Ah, what a sad
    moment!)

But the wind has left its echo
floating on the rivers.

The world of fireflies
has invaded my memory.

    (Ah, what a pretty
    moment!)

And a tiny heart
blossoms on my fingers.

    *

On the pool, the lotuses
of concentric circles.
On my temples I bear
the majesty of silence.

Marvelous bevels
make the poplars shiver.
White snails are moving
along the grassy bank.

How lovely and how sad the Carrera del Darro must be, and what clouds there must be over Valparaíso! I remember Granada the way one remembers a dead fiancée or a day of sunshine from childhood. Have all of the leaves fallen?

FROM A LETTER TO EMILIA LLANOS MEDINA,
NOVEMBER 28, 1920

Granada: Paradise Closed to Many

Granada loves tiny things, and so does the rest of Andalusia. Popular speech places even verbs in the diminutive, making it easier to trust and love. But the diminutives one hears in Malaga and Seville are but charm and rhythm. Seville and Malaga are cities on the crossroads of the water, cities that thirst for adventure and slip away to sea. Granada, tranquil and refined, girded by her sierras, riding eternally at anchor, sets her own horizons, takes pleasure in her small jewels, and offers her bland diminutive: a diminutive without rhythm, almost without grace and charm when one compares it with the phonetic dance of Malaga and Seville, but cordial, domestic, affectionate. A diminutive frightened as a bird, one which opens secret chambers of feeling and reveals the subtlest, best-defined nuances of the city.

The diminutive's only mission is to limit, enclose, bring indoors and place in our hands objects and ideas which seem too large: time and space, the sea, the moon, distances, and even action.

We don't want the world to be so big, the sea so deep. We need to limit and domesticate anything huge.

Granada cannot leave her house. She isn't like other cities, which are on the edge of the ocean or of great rivers: cities that travel and return enriched by what they have seen. Lonely and pure, Granada grows smaller and binds up her extraordinary soul. Her only escape is her high natural port of stars. And thus, with no thirst for adventure, she doubles back upon herself, using the diminutive to rein in her imagination, just as she reins in her body to avoid excessive flight, and soberly harmonizes her interiors with the living architecture that lies around her.

In a word, the true aesthetic of Granada is the aesthetic of the diminutive, of tiny things, and her true creations are the little chamber, the mirador of lovely, small proportions, the small garden or statue.

The so-called artistic "schools" of Granada are groups of artists who work lovingly on small-scale works. They do other things, of course, but it is this type of work that best reveals their personality.

One might say that the schools of Granada, her most perfect representatives, are given to preciosity. The tradition of the arabesque of the Alhambra, complicated and small in scope, weighs on every great artist in the city. The palace of the Alhambra – a palace which Andalusian fantasy looked at through the wrong end of the telescope – has always been the aesthetic axis of the city. Granada seems never to have realized that the palace of Carlos V and the well-drawn cathedral rise in her midst. There is no Caesarean tradition, no tradition of the massive column or clustered pier. She is still frightened by the great, cold cathedral tower, and withdraws into her ancient little rooms, with a pot of myrtle and a stream of cold water, to carve little ivory flowers, inlaying them in hard wood.

When the Renaissance tradition comes to the city, Granada simply flees, or, mocking its grand dimensions, constructs the unlikely little tower of Santa Ana: tiny tower more fit for doves than for bells, made with all the elegance and ancient charm of Granada.

In years when the triumphal arch is reborn, Alonso Cano is carving his little virgins, precious examples of virtue and intimacy. When the Castilian tongue is mature enough to describe the elements of nature and supple enough for the most poignant mystical constructs, Fray Luis de Granada gives us his delectable descriptions of small objects and things.

It is Fray Luis who, in his *Introduction to the Symbol of the Faith*, tells how God's wisdom and providence shine more brightly in small things than in large ones. Humble, reserved, a "preciosista," he is a master of the loving look, like all good people of Granada.

When Gongora issues his proclamation on behalf of pure, abstract poetry – a proclamation taken up avidly by all the most lyrical spirits of his day – Granada reappears on the literary map of Spain. Soto de Rojas takes the difficult, exacting orders of Góngora. But while the subtle Cordovan poet toys with oceans, forests, and the elements, Soto de Rojas encloses himself in his garden and discovers water jets, dahlias, finches and gentle breezes. Moorish, half-Italian breezes rustle the boughs and fruits and thickets of his poetry.

In a word: what characterizes him is his preciosity. He orders his nature instinctively, as though decorating a room. He flees from the great elements of Nature and prefers the garlands and fruit baskets he can make with his own hands. That is what has always happened in Granada. Beneath the impression made by the Renaissance, native blood was pulsing, producing its virginal fruit.

The aesthetic of small things is our most distinctive trait, the very most delicate play of our artists. It is not a matter of patience but of time; not of work but a labor of virtue and love. This could happen in no other city.

*

Granada is a city of leisure, a city for contemplation and fantasy, a city where, better than in any other, the lover can write on the ground the name of his beloved. The hours are longer, more delectable in Granada than in any other city in Spain. There are complicated sunsets with unheard-of colors that seem to go on forever.

We carry on long conversations with friends in the middle of the street.

Granada lives on fantasy. It is full of initiatives, but short on action.

Only in a city of leisure and tranquility could there be such exquisite tasters of waters, of temperatures, of sunsets.

Her people are surrounded by the most splendid nature imaginable, but they do not go to it.

The landscapes are extraordinary, but the person from Granada prefers to look at them from his window. He is frightened of the elements, and feels scorn for the noisy rabble. Because he is a man of fantasy, he has little courage. He prefers his own gentle snow-cooled breeze to the terrible, harsh wind heard in Ronda, for example, and he is ready to place his entire soul in the diminutive and bring the world into his room. Wisely, he realizes that he can understand it better that way. He renounces adventure, travel, the curiosities of other lands. Most of the time he rejects luxury, fine clothes, the city.

He scorns all this and makes his garden more beautiful. He retires into himself, a man of few friends (isn't the reserve of Granada proverbial in the rest of Andalusia?)

He stares lovingly at the objects around him. He is in no hurry. Perhaps this is why the artists of Granada have taken such pleasure in carving small things or describing worlds of reduced dimensions. Someone will say that these traits lead to philosophizing, but philosophy demands a certain constancy, a mathematical equilibrium that is rather difficult in Granada. Granada is fit for dream and daydream, and it borders everywhere on the ineffable. Besides, there is a great difference between dreaming and thinking, although they begin with similar attitudes. Granada will always be more plastic than philosophical, more lyrical than dramatical. Her tender personality is hidden away inside her houses and her landscape. Her voice comes down from a little mirador, or rises from a dark window. Impersonal, poignant voice, full of ineffable aristocratic melancholy. Who is singing? Where does it come from, that slender voice, night and day at the same time?

To hear that voice, one must enter the tiny chambers and corners of the city, live the city's unpeopled interior and well-girded solitude. And, what is even more admirable, explore one's own intimacy, one's own secret, taking a definitively lyrical perspective on things.

One must make oneself a little poorer, forget one's name, renounce what people call "personality."

Just the opposite of Seville. Seville is man in the full complexity of his sensuality and emotion. It is political intrigue and the triumphal arch. Don Pedro and Don Juan. It is full of the human element, and its voice brings tears, because anyone can understand it. Granada is like the narration of what already happened in Seville.

There is the emptiness of something that is gone forever.

When one understands the intimate, cautious soul of the city – soul of the interior, of the small garden – one can also explain the aesthetics and techniques of many of our most representative artists.

Everything has a sweet domestic air. And yet, who can understand, who can penetrate this intimacy? The poet Pedro Soto de Rojas defined it in the seventeenth century. Returning from Madrid, full of sorrow and disenchantment, he wrote on the cover of one of his books these words, giving the most exact definition possible of Granada: "Paradise Closed to Many."

Paquito is going to Oxford in October... I imagine him as an Englishman — very serious, very elegant, with that air of a wild duck that all those strange, insular people have. You and I will remain in Spain: billy goat, rooster, bull, fiery auroras, the white light of courtyards, where the humidity spots the heartless old walls with incredible shades of green. If only you could see Andalusia! When you walk you have to open galleries in the golden light, like the moles in their dark world. The brilliant silks Michaelangelize the fannies of well-to-do women, the roosters nail their banderillas into the shoulders of the dawn, and I turn brown from the sun and from the full moon.

FROM A LETTER TO PEPÍN BELLO,
JULY 1925

August.
Against the sunset
peaches and sugar,
and the sun inside the afternoon
like the stone in a fruit.

The ear of corn is holding
its hard, yellow laughter.

August.
Children eat
dark bread and tasty moon.

Evening

(Was my Lucy dangling
her feet in the stream?)

Three huge poplars
and a star.

The silence bitten
by frogs resembles
a gauze painted
with green polka dots.

In the river
a dry tree
flowers
into concentric circles.

On the waters I have dreamed
the dark little girl of Granada.

Ballad of the Three Rivers

The river Guadalquivir
passes through olive and orange trees.
The two rivers of Granada
descend from the snow to the wheat.

Ah, love
that went away forever!

The river Guadalquivir
has garnet-colored beards.
The two rivers of Granada,
one blood, the other tears.

Ah, love
that fled on the breeze!

For sailing ships
Seville has a path.
In the water of Granada
only sighs can row.

Ah, love
that went away forever!

Guadalquivir, high tower
and wind in the orange groves.
Dauro and Genil, little towers
dead in the pools below.

Ah, love
that fled on the breeze!

Who doubts that the water carries
a will-o'-the-wisp of screams?

Ah, love
that went away forever!

It carries olives and orange blossoms,
Andalusia, to your seas.

Ah, love
that fled on the breeze!

Tree, tree,
dry and green.

The girl with the pretty face
is picking olives.
The wind, suitor of towers,
takes her by the waist.

Four riders went by
on Andalusian ponies,
with suits of blue and green,
and long, dark capes.

"Come to Córdoba, girl."
The girl does not listen.

Three little bullfighters pass,
with slender waists
in bright orange suits
and swords of old silver.

"Come to Seville, girl."
The girl does not listen.

When the evening turned
mauve with scattered light
a boy came by carrying
roses and moonlit myrtle.

"Come to Granada, girl."
And the girl does not listen.

The girl with the pretty face
goes on picking olives,
the gray arm of the wind
wrapped around her waist.

Tree, tree,
dry and green.

St. Michael

(Granada)

TO DIEGO BUIGAS DE DALMÁU

You can see them from the railings
on the mount, the mount, the mount,
mules and shadows of mules
carrying sunflower seed.

Their eyes, in the shady places,
cloud over with huge night.
The salty dawn is rustling
in river-bends of breeze.

A sky of white mules
closes its quicksilver eyes,
making the calm penumbra
a resting place for hearts.
And the water turns cold
so no one will touch it.
Crazy, uncovered water
on the mount, the mount, the mount.

*

St. Michael, full of lace
in the alcove of his tower
shows his lovely thighs
ringed in lantern light.

Domesticated archangel
pointing to twelve o'clock
feigns a sweet anger
of feathers and nightingales.
St. Michael sings in the glass,
ephebe of three thousand nights,
fragrant with cologne
and far away from flowers.

          *

On the beach the sea is dancing
a poem of balconies.
The shores of the moon
gain voices and lose reeds.
Women in bright costume
are eating sunflower seeds,
their huge bottoms hidden
like copper planets.
Tall gentlemen come by
and ladies of sad mien,
dusky with nostalgia
for a yesterday of nightingales.
And the Bishop of Manila,
saffron-blind and poor,
says a double-bladed mass
for the men and women.

          *

St. Michael was resting calmly
in the alcove of his tower,
his petticoats frozen
in spangles and lace.

St. Michael, king of balloons
and of uneven numbers,
in the berberesque grace
of shouts and miradors.

Sleepwalking Ballad

FOR GLORIA GINER AND FERNANDO DE LOS RÍOS

Green I want you green.
Green wind, green boughs.
The ship on the sea
and the horse on the mountain.
With shadow at her waist
she dreams at her railing,
green flesh, green hair,
and eyes of cold silver.
Green I want you green.
Under the gypsy moon
things are looking at her,
and she cannot return their gaze.

*

Green I want you green.
Great stars of frost
come with the shadow-fish
that opens the way for dawn.
The fig tree rubs its wind
with the sandpaper of its branches,
and the hill, a wildcat,
bristles with bitter cactus.
But who will come? From where?
She remains at her railing,
green flesh, green hair,
dreaming of the bitter sea.

"Compadre, I want to trade
my horse for your house,
my saddle for your mirror,
my knife for your blanket.
Compadre, I've come here bleeding
from the passes of Cabra."
"If I could, young man,
that deal would be done.
But I am no longer I,
and my house is no longer mine."
"Compadre, I want to die
decently in bed.
A steel one, if I can,
with the best linen sheets.
Don't you see this wound
from my chest to my throat?"
"Three hundred brown roses
cover your white shirt.
Your blood oozes and smells
around your sash.
But I am no longer I,
and my house is no longer mine."
"Let me climb, at least,
up to the high railings.
Let me climb! Let me,
up to the high rails!
Big railings of the moon
where the water roars."

*

The two compadres climb
up to the high railing.
Leaving a trail of blood.
Leaving a trail of tears.
Little tin-leaf lanterns
tremble on the rooftops.
A thousand crystal tambourines
were wounding the dawn.

*

Green I want you green,
green wind, green boughs.
The two compadres climbed.
The long wind was leaving
a strange taste in their mouth
of basil, gall and mint.
"Compadre, where is she?
Where is your bitter girl?"
"How often she awaited you,
how often did she wait,
fresh face, black hair
upon this rail of green!"

*

Over the face of the rain-well
the gypsy girl was rocking.
Green flesh, green hair
and eyes of cold silver.
An icicle of the moon
holds her over the water.

The night became as intimate
as a little village square.
Drunken Civil Guards
were knocking at the door.
Green I want you green.
Green wind. Green boughs.
The ship on the sea.
And the horse on the mountain.

I wish I could be with you to enjoy the spring air of Granada, the pagan odor of the temples, the green gusts of wind sent by the Vega, dressed as a bride by the bean vines in blossom.

FROM A LETTER TO EDUARDO RODRÍGUEZ VALDIVIESO,

APRIL 8, 1933

Holy Week in Granada

The untroubled traveler, full of smiles and the screams of locomotives, goes to the carnival of Valencia. The bacchant goes to the Holy Week of Seville. The man burning for nudes goes to Malaga. But the melancholy, contemplative man goes to Granada, in order to be alone with a breeze of sweet basil, dark moss, and trilling nightingales. To be alone with the breeze that comes from the old hills of the Alhambra – from the bonfire of saffron, deep gray, and blotting-paper pink of its walls. To be alone. To ponder an atmosphere full of difficult voices, in an air so beautiful it is almost thought, at a nerve center of Spain where the "meseta" poetry of St. John of the Cross fills with cedars, cinnamons, and fountains, and Spanish mysticism can receive that Oriental air, that "wounded stag" (wounded by love) who "comes to the hill."

To be alone: to have the solitude one would want in Florence. To understand not the water's play, as at Versailles, but the water's passion, the water's agony.

Or to be with one's beloved and feel the springtime pulsing in the trees and in the skin of the delicate marble columns and see how the yellow orbs of the lemons climb through the glades and push back the frightened snow.

Whoever wants to feel the sweet ticktock of blood in his lips, and feel the stamina of the bull, should be off to the baroque tumult of universal Seville. But whoever would like to sit down at a café table among phantasms and perhaps find a wonderful old ring somewhere along the corridors of his heart should go to the inner, hidden

Granada. He will soon be surprised to learn that there is no Holy Week in Granada. Holy Week does not suit the Christian, antispectacular spirit of her people. When I was a child I sometimes went to the Holy Burial. But only a few times, for the rich people of Granada did not always want to spend money on that parade.

These past few years, out of commercialism, they have put on processions wholly devoid of the seriousness and poetry of the Holy Week I knew as a child. Back then it was a Holy Week of lace, of canaries flying amid the tapers, of an air that was lukewarm and sad, as if the whole day had fallen asleep on the opulent throats of the old maids who promenaded on Holy Thursday pining for some soldier, judge, or foreign professor to carry them far, far away.

In those days the entire city was like a slow merry-go-round moving in and out of fantastically beautiful churches that were both fun-houses and the apotheosis of the theater. Some of the altars were sown with wheat, others had little cascades, and some had the tenderness and poverty of a shooting gallery at the village fair. This one was nothing but reeds, like a celestial henhouse of firecrackers, and that one was immense, with the cruel purple, the sumptuous ermine of the poetry of Calderón.

In a house on the Calle de la Colcha, the street where wreaths and coffins were sold to poor people, those dressed as Roman soldiers would gather for practice. These "soldiers" were not a formal confraternity like the saucy *armaos* of the marvelous Sevillian neighborhood of the Macarena. They were hired hands – moving men, bootblacks, sick people just out of the hospital in need of a few pesetas. They put on the red beards of

Schopenhauer or of flaming cats or ferocious professors. The captain was a military technician, and he taught them to mark the rhythm, which went like this – *porón… chas!* – and they would strike the ground with their lances in a deliciously comical way. As an example of Granada's natural genius, I will tell you that one year the Roman soldiers did very poorly at rehearsal and spent more than fifteen days furiously striking their lances on the ground before they could do so in unison. And then the captain shouted desperately, "Enough! Enough! If you go on like this we'll end up carrying the lances in candleholders!" A saying very characteristic of Granada, and already commented on by several generations.

I would like to ask Granada to restore that old-fashioned Holy Week and have the good taste to hide that hideous procession of the Last Supper and not profane the Alhambra – which is not and never will be Christian – with the jangle of processions where false elegance mocks good taste and the crowd breaks laurels, tramples on violets, and urinates by the hundred on the illustrious walls of poetry.

Granada must save for herself and for the traveler her inner Holy Week, one so intimate and so silent that, as I remember, a startled breeze from the Vega would enter the city by the Calle de la Gracia and would reach the fountain in the Plaza Nueva without hearing a single noise or song.

That way Granada's snowy spring will be perfect, and through this festival the intelligent traveler will be able to converse with her classic types: the human ocean of Ganivet, whose eyes are on the secret lilies of the Darro; the watcher of sunsets who climbs anxiously to the rooftop; the fellow who loves the Sierra as a form, without ever having gone near it; the dark beauty who yearns for love and sits by her mother in the garden; a whole admirable town of contemplatives who are surrounded by unique natural beauty, want nothing, and only know how to smile.

Amid an incredible variety of forms, landscapes, light and aromas, the uninformed traveler will get the feeling that Granada is the capital of a kingdom with its own art and literature, and will find a curious mixture of Jewish and Moorish Granada which will seem to have been blended by Christianity but are really alive and incorruptible in their ignorance.

Neither the prodigious mound of the cathedral nor the great imperial and Roman stamp of Carlos V have effaced the little shop of the Jew who prays before an image recast from a menorah, just as the sepulchers of the Catholic Kings have not kept the crescent from showing at times on the chest of Granada's finest sons. The dark struggle continues, without being expressed. Well, not without expression, because on the Colina Roja are two dead palaces, the Alhambra and the palace of Carlos V, which continue to fight the fatal duel that throbs in the heart of each of Granada's citizens.

All this the traveler should look at when he gets to Granada, which at this very moment is putting on her long dress of springtime. As for the caravans of noisy tourists who like cabarets and luxury hotels – those frivolous groups that the people on the Albaicín call "Tío Turista" – to them the city's soul is closed.

In Madrid the autumn has been delightful. With true melancholy I remember the great yellow treetops in the Plaza de Campillo, and that solitary Plaza de los Lobos, full of acacia leaves, and the divine, first cold wind which sends a shiver through the fountain in the Plaza Nueva. All of this is the Granada of my dreams and my loneliness, when I was an adolescent and no one had yet loved me.

FROM A LETTER TO EDUARDO RODRÍGUEZ VALDIVIESO,
OCTOBER OR NOVEMBER, 1932

Casida of One Wounded by Water

I want to go down to the well,
I want to climb the walls of Granada,
to look at the heart pierced
by the dark awl of the waters.

The wounded boy was moaning
with a crown of frost.
Pools, cisterns and fountains
lifted their swords in the air.
Oh, what a fury of love, what a wounding edge,
what nocturnal murmur, what white death!
What deserts of light were sinking
the sandbacks of early morning!
The boy was all alone.
The city drowsed in his throat.
A water jet that comes from dreams
defends him from the hungry algae.
The boy and his agony, face to face,
were two green rains entwined.
The boy lay flat on the earth,
and his agony made a curve.

I want to go down to the well,
I want to die my death by the mouthful.
I want to fill my heart with moss,
to see the boy wounded by the water.

Casida of the Boughs

Through the groves of Tamarit
the dogs of lead have come
to wait for the boughs to fall,
to wait for them to break by themselves.

The Tamarit has an apple tree
with an apple of sobs.
A nightingale snuffs out sighs
and a pheasant chases them through the dust.

But the boughs are happy,
the branches are like us.
They do not think of the rain and like trees
they have suddenly fallen asleep.

Seated with the water on their knees
two valleys were waiting for autumn.
The dusk, with the tread of an elephant,
was pushing the treetrunks and branches.

In the groves of the Tamarit
there are many boys with veiled faces,
waiting for my boughs to fall,
waiting for them to break by themselves.

Ghazal of the Love Which Hides from Sight

Just to hear
the bell of the Vela,
I gave you a crown of verbena.

Granada was a moon
drowned in the ivy.

Just to hear
the bell of the Vela,
I tore up my garden of Cartagena.

Granada was a doe,
pink among the weathervanes.

Just to hear
the bell of the Vela
I burned in your body
without knowing whose it was.

Ghazal of the Dead Child

Every afternoon in Granada,
every afternoon a child dies.
Every afternoon the water sits down
to converse with its friends.

The dead wear wings of moss.
The clouded wind and clean wind
are two pheasants that fly around the towers
and the day is a wounded boy.

No blade of lark remained in the air
when I found you in the wine caverns.
No crumb of cloud remained on the earth
when you were drowning in the river.

A giant of water fell upon the hills
and the valley went tumbling, with dogs and iris.
Your body, in the violet shadow of my hands,
dead on the bank, was an archangel of cold.

Ghazal of the Morning Market Place

Through the gate of Elvira
I want to see you pass,
to learn your name
and break into tears.

What grey moon at nine o'clock
drained your cheek of blood?
Who collects your seed,
aflame in the snow?
What little cactus needle
murders your crystal…?

Through the gateway of Elvira
I want to see you pass,
to drink your eyes
and break into tears.

What a voice, to punish me,
you raise in the market place!
What an estranged carnation
in the mounds of wheat!
How far I am when with you,
how close when you depart!

Through the gateway of Elvira
I want to see you pass,
to feel your thighs
and break into tears.

Autumn turns the Vega into a submerged bay. In the ramparts of the Alhambra… haven't you ever felt the desire to embark? Haven't you seen the spectral little boats that nod sleepily at the foot of its towers? Today I realize, in the midst of this gray, mother-of-pearl sunset, that I live in a marvellous Atlantis.

I am eager to leave [for Madrid], and yet, I don't want to depart until everything has turned completely golden. Now, in autumn, the valleys of the Darro and the Genil are the only paths in the world that lead directly to the land of Noplace, *lost somewhere in those murmuring mists.*

I am neither happy nor sad, I am inside the autumn; I am…

> *Ay, heart, heart*
> *Cupid's St. Sebastian!*

FROM A LETTER TO MELCHOR FERNÁNDEZ ALMAGRO,
NOVEMBER 1921

How a City Sings from November to November

Like a boy gazing in wonder at his mother dressed in bright colors for a party, I want to show you the city where I was born, the city of Granada. To do so, I want to give you examples of her music, and I will have to sing them. That will be difficult, for I do not sing like a professional but like a poet, or rather as the farm boy sings while goading along his oxen. My voice is weak, my throat delicate; so please do not be surprised if you hear me let out one of those false notes known in our language as "roosters." If one escapes, at least it won't be the corrosive "rooster" of professional singers, terrible bird that pecks at their eyes and ruins their glory. I will turn it into a little silver rooster, and lovingly place it upon the sweet neck of the most melancholy girl in this room, here in Montevideo.

A man from Granada blind from birth and absent from his city for many years would know the season by what he heard sung in the streets. We are not going to take our eyes on this little visit. We shall leave them on a plate of snow, so that St. Lucy won't feel quite so proud.

Why must we always use only our sight, and never our smell or taste to study a city? The special pastries, the *alfajor*, the *torta alajú*, the *mantecado* of Laujar, tell us quite as much about Granada as do its glazed tiles or Moorish arches. And the marzipan of Toledo with its monstrous vestment of plums and anise pearls, invented by a cook of Carlos V, speaks more poignantly of the Emperor's Germanic origins than does his ruddy chin. While a cathedral remains fastened to its own epoch, its profile slowly crumbling away, eternally unable to step into the next day, a song leaps suddenly from its epoch into ours, live and nervous as a frog, with its fresh melancholy or fresh happiness, as miraculous as the seed that flowers when taken from the Pharaoh's tomb. So then, let us *hear* the city of Granada.

The year has four seasons, namely winter, spring, summer and autumn.

Granada has two rivers, eighty bell towers, four thousand irrigation ditches, fifty fountains, a thousand and one jets of water, and one hundred thousand inhabitants. It has a factory where they make guitars and bandurrias, a store where they sell pianos and accordions and harmonicas and especially drums. It has two promenades for singing – the Paseo del Salón and the Paseo del Alhambra – and one for crying, the Alameda de los Tristes, true acme of all European Romanticism, and it has a legion of pyrotechnicians who build towers of noise, with an art equal to that of the Court of the Lions, to irritate the square water of the reflecting ponds.

The Sierra Nevada lends a background of boulders or of snow or of green dream to the songs that cannot fly: songs that fall upon the rooftops or burn their little hands in the hot earth, or drown in the dry spikes of July wheat.

Those songs are the physiognomy of the city, and in them we shall feel its rhythm and temperature.

Using our hearing and our sense of smell, we draw closer, and our first sensation is the smell of sedge, of mint, of a vegetable world gently crushed under the hoofs of the mules and horses and oxen that criss-cross the Vega. And then, the rhythm of the water. But not mad water that goes wherever it wants. Water with tempo, rather than murmur, water that is well-measured and precise as it follows its geometrical, rhythmic course through the irrigation ditches. Water that irrigates and sings here below, and water that suffers and weeps, full of tiny white violins, on the hill of the Generalife.

There is no play of water in Granada: that is left for Versailles where the water is a spectacle and where it is as abundant as the sea: proud mechanical architecture with no sense of song. The water of Granada slakes our thirst. It is living water that becomes part of whoever drinks it or hears it or wants to die in it. It suffers a passion of *jets d'eau* and lies down to die in the reflecting pool. Juan Ramón Jiménez has said it like this:

> What pain and what despair
> at being led about!
> And what somnambulistic
> repetition as
> she reaches the last corner!
> What banging of her head
> against the final walls!
> The water falls asleep and dreams
> of being stripped of tears!

There are also two valleys. Two rivers. In them the water no longer sings; it is a deaf murmur, a mist that mingles with the windspouts sent down by the Sierra. The Genil, crowned with poplars, and the Dauro, crowned with lilies.

But everything is exactly right, everything has human proportion. Air and water in just the right tiny doses. This is the distinction, the special charm of Granada: things for inside the room. Small courtyard, small music, small water, air to dance on our fingertips.

The Cantabrian Sea or the high wind that hurls itself over the cliffs at Ronda frighten the Granadan who peers out the window that frames and defines him. The air grows tame and so does the water, for when the elements come to a boil they smash the tonic of the human scale and annihilate, exhaust the personality of man, who cannot master them and who has to let go of his landscape and his dream. The Granadan sees things through the wrong end of the binoculars. That is why Granada never produced any heroes. That is why Boabdil, the most famous Granadan ever, surrendered her to the Castilians. And that is why, in every age, the Granadan has withdrawn into his tiny chambers, with only the moon for decoration.

Granada is made for music, for it is a city enclosed by mountain ranges, where the melody is returned and polished and blocked by walls and boulders. Music is for cities away from the coast. Seville and Malaga and Cadiz escape through their ports, but Granada's only way out is its high natural port of stars. Granada is withdrawn, enclosed, apt for rhythm and the echo, the marrow of music.

Her highest expression is not poetical but musical, with a wide avenue that leads to mysticism. And so she does not have, as does Seville (city of Don Juan, city of love), a dramatical expression, but a lyrical one. And while Seville reaches its heights in Lope and Tirso and in Beaumarchais and Zorrilla and in the prose of Bécquer, Granada reaches hers in an orchestra of water jets charged with Andalusian pain, and in Narvaez's music for the *vihuela*, and in Falla and in Debussy. And while in Seville the human element dominates the landscape, and Don Pedro and Don Alonso and Duke Octavio of Naples and Figaro and Mañara stroll through closed spaces, in Granada phantasms stroll through the two empty palaces, and the spur turns into a slow ant racing across an endless marble pavement, and the love letter turns into a fistful of grass, and the sword turns into a delicate mandolin that only spiders and nightingales are unafraid to play.

We have arrived in Granada toward the end of November. It smells like burnt straw, and the piles of leaves are beginning to rot. It is raining and people are indoors. But in the middle of the Puerta Real there are already a few stalls selling noisemakers (*zambombas*). The Sierra is covered with clouds, and there is room enough here for all the music of northern Spain. A girl from Armilla or Santa Fe or Atarfe, a servant, buys a *zambomba* and sings this song:

> Of the four muleteers
> who go to the water,
> the one with the grey mule
> steals my heart.
>
> Of the four muleteers
> who go to the river,
> the one with the grey mule
> is my husband.
>
> Why do you look for warmth
> farther up the street
> if your face
> is glowing with heat?

This is the folk rhythm that is heard all over the Vega, and which the Moors carried from Granada to Africa. Today in Tunis they play it like this. [*He plays*].

The song of the four muleteers is sung beside the glowing embers of beanstalks burnt for heat in the numerous villages outside Granada, the crown of villages that climbs into the Sierra.

But December advances, the sky is clear, flocks of turkeys arrive, and the sound of tambourines and chicharras takes over the city. At night, from inside the closed houses, one goes on hearing the same rhythm. It comes out the windows and the chimneys, as though born directly from the earth. The voices climb a little higher, the streets fill with brightly-lit booths, with huge mounds of apples, the bells of midnight join the little bells that the nuns ring at daybreak, the Alhambra grows darker and more remote than ever, the hens abandon their eggs on the frosty straw. By now the nuns of the Convent of Santo Tomás de Villanueva are putting a flat, yellow hat on St. Joseph and a mantilla, with its curved comb, on the Virgin Mary. By now the clay sheep, the little woollen dogs are climbing the stairs toward the artificial moss.

The sound of *carrañacas* begins to be heard and amid castanets and potcovers, graters and copper mortars, they sing the joyous Christmas ballad of the two pilgrims:

> Two pilgrims
> are going to Rome
> so the Pope can marry them,
> for they are cousins.

The young man is wearing
a hat of oilcloth,
the pilgrim girl
a velvet one.

While they were crossing
Victoria Bridge
the bridesmaid stumbled,
the bride fell down.

They have come to the palace
and go upstairs.
In the Pope's chambers
they discourage them.

The Pope has asked
what are their names.
He says Pedro,
and Ana, she.

The Pope has asked
how old they are.
She says fifteen,
seventeen, he.

The Pope has asked
where they are from.
She says from Cabra,
Antequera, he.

The Pope has asked
if they have sinned.

Yes, he answers,
he has given her a kiss.

The pilgrim girl
is rather shy.
Her face has turned
red as a rose!

The Pope has replied
from inside his room:
"Wish *I* were a pilgrim
and could do the same!"

The bells of Rome
are pealing now,
for at last the pilgrims
are married.

People sing this song on the streets in bacchic throngs,
little children sing it with their nannies, and so do drunken
prostitutes behind the closed curtains of their carriages,
and soldiers remembering their home towns as they have
their pictures taken by the balustrade along the Genil. It is
the gaiety of the streets, the humor of Andalusia, the subtle
refinement and wit of a people steeped in culture.

But we leave the streets and head for the Jewish neighborhood, and find it deserted. We hear this song full of
hidden melancholy, the opposite of "The Little Pilgrims."

Just who is singing this song? It is Granada's very
purest voice, her elegiac voice, the clash of East and West
in the two broken palaces that are full of ghosts, the Palace
of Charles V and the Alhambra:

> Down the street
> goes the man I love.
> I can't see his face
> under his hat.
>
> A curse on the hat
> that covers all that!
> I'll buy him a new one
> for Christmas.

The last Christmas carol scurries away, and the city falls asleep in the ices of January.

In February, with the sun shining and giving us fresh air, people go on picnics and hang swings from the olive trees, and one hears the same cry – the same *uyuí* – as in the mountains of northern Spain.

People are singing on the outskirts of Granada, where the water is still hidden under a thin layer of ice. The grown boys stretch out on the ground to see the legs of the girls on the swings, the older ones peeping at them from the corners of their eyes. The air is still cold.

The streets in the poor, outlying neighborhoods are calm now. A dog or two, a breeze from the olive groves, and suddenly, *plop!* Somebody tosses a pail of dirty water out the door. But the olive groves are full of life:

> The girl is swinging,
> her lover is watching,
> and he says, "My darling,
> this rope won't hold."

This rope won't hold.
Where will she land?
In the last little alleys
of San Nicolás.

Some of these songs have all the purity of the folksongs of the fifteenth century:

I go to the olive groves,
I go in the evenings,
to see how the air
is moving the leaf.
To see how the air
is moving the leaf.

This is the same as that marvelous song of 1560, with a
melody by Juan Vázquez, that says:

I come from the poplars, mother,
to see them moving in the breeze.

From the poplars of Seville,
from seeing my sweet friend.

From the poplars of Granada,
from seeing my beloved.

To see them moving in the breeze,
I come from the poplars, mother.

The purest classical reminiscences enliven these songs
of the olive groves. And this is not at all rare in Spain

where songs by Juan del Encina, Salinas, Fuenllana, and Pisador turn up suddenly in Galicia or Avila, sung in all their purity.

At nightfall people come home from the olive groves and often the gatherings go on indoors.

But when spring arrives and leaves are beginning to bud and balconies begin to open, the landscape is strangely transformed. We have come down from the snow, down to the laurel tree and all the sharp profiles of the south.

Children have already begun to play in the streets, and in my childhood a popular old poet whom they used to call "Look-at-the-Sky" would come outside and sit on a bench in the park. Casks of new wine are arriving from the coast, and at twilight the city sings this song heralding the bullfights, a song with a form as pure as the air of the last day of March:

> In the Café de Chinitas
> Paquiro said to his brother:
> I'm so much braver than you,
> more *torero*, more of a Gypsy.
>
> Paquiro took out his watch
> and this is what he said:
> "This bull must die
> by four-thirty this afternoon."
>
> When it struck four in the tower
> they left the café,
> and Paquiro went strutting about
> like a big-name bullfighter.

But what's this, what's going on? Two women friends from one of the villages meet at the Humilladero gate, through which the Catholic Monarchs entered Granada:

> Comadre, where are you coming from?
> Comadre, from Granada.
> Comadre, what's happening there?
> Comadre, nothing at all:
> they're making the same old baskets
> and ringing the same old bells.

In May and June the bells of Granada ring incessantly. The students cannot study. In the Plaza de Bibarrambla, the cathedral bells – bells that seem to ring underwater, with seaweed and clouds – make it impossible for the farmers to hear one another. The church bells of San Juan de Dios hurl through the air their Baroque reredos of lamentation and banging bronze. The Alhambra is lonelier and more forlorn than ever, dead and flayed, alien to the city, more and more remote. But there are ice cream vendors in the streets, and stalls with raisin bread with sesame seeds, and men selling honey bars with garbanzo beans.

Along come the dragon and dwarfs of Corpus Christi, and in the streets Granada's women, with their lovely naked arms and wombs like dark magnolias, suddenly open their green, orange, blue parasols, in the frenzy of lights and violins and carriages, in a carousel of love, gallantry and nostalgia, in the Castle-of-No-Return of the fireworks.

From the Vega comes a swarm of whistles (sold at the village fairs), and on the Calle de Elvira, most ancient

Elvira Street
where the *manolas* live,
the ones that go up to the Alhambra
by twos and threes, alone...

we hear this song, so expressive of Granada:

Under the leaf
of the vervain
my lover is sick,
Jesus, how sad!

Under the leaf
of the lettuce
my lover is sick
with a fever.

Under the leaf
of the parsley
my lover is sick,
I'll stay by his side.

The last firecracker, the so-called "thunderbolt," is
shot off, and in a single day all Granada leaves for the
country. The city is abandoned to summer, which comes in
an hour. The ladies cover their armchairs with white drop-
cloths and close the doors of the balcony. Those who stay
behind are living in the courtyards and in the downstairs
rooms sitting in their rockers and drinking cool water from
the wet red clay of the water jugs. One begins to think and
to live by night. And this is the time when the city sings,
to the accompaniment of guitars, those *fandangos* and

granadinas that are so peculiar and have such a depth of landscape.

The whole of traditional balladry comes to the lips of the children. The most beautiful ballads, unmatched by any Romantic poet, the bloodiest legends, the most unexpected plays on words. Among countless examples I have chosen this one, sung by the children in some of the villages and by the boys who live around the Plaza Larga in the Albaicín. In the August night, no one can resist this tender melody. It is the ballad of the Duke of Alba:

> "It is rumored, it is rumored,
> it is rumored in Seville
> that the Duke is getting married
> to another, and forgetting you."

> "Let him marry if he wants.
> Why should I care?"
> "You ought to care, sister,
> for your honor is lost."
> She went upstairs to a room
> where she used to embroider and sew.
> Now she goes to a window
> that overlooks the square.
> She sees the Duke coming
> with another woman.
> She makes him a secret sign,
> to see if he will catch it.
> "What does Ana, Ana want?
> What can she want, this Ana María?"
> "Duke of Alba, Duke of Alba,
> Duke of Alba of my life,

they tell me you are marrying
a lady of great worth."
"Who told you that? Who told you
the truth and not a lie?
The wedding is tomorrow,
I was coming to invite you."
When she heard those words,
she fell dead to the ground.
Doctors and surgeons
hurried to her side.
They tried to open her breast
to see why she was dying.
To one side of her heart
she had two slips of gold.
One of them said "Duke,"
the other, "of my life."
"If only I had known
that you loved me so,
I would not have forgotten you,
dove of my soul."

But it is time now for us to tiptoe down a certain road of red clay, bordered by prickly pears, to a gathering in a remote corner of the hills. They are singing and dancing. We hear guitars, castanets and rustic instruments, tambourines and triangles. These are the people who sing the *roas* and *alboreás*, the *cachuchas* and the *ʒorongo*, which has greatly influenced the music of Manuel de Falla. [*He plays*]

In the hills the yellow light of dawn brings us the songs of reapers and threshers. But those rural songs never enter the city.

September. The air is nippy. The wheel is coming full circle.

> Round and round we go,
> and autumn appears in the poplar groves.

And so do the village fairs. The fairs, with walnuts, jujubes, red haws, crowds of quinces, towers of sugar bread and tarts from the Corzo pastry shop.

St. Michael on his hill brandishes his sword, surrounded by sunflowers. Remember my ballad?

> St. Michael full of lace
> in the alcove of his tower
> shows his lovely thighs
> ringed in lantern light...
>
> St. Michael, king of balloons
> and of uneven numbers
> in the Berberesque grace
> of screams and miradors.

Berberesque grace of screams and miradors. That is Granada, seen from the Cerro del Aceituno. The song one hears is chaotic. It is all Granada singing at once: rivers, voices, ropes, foliage, processions, an ocean of fruits, the music of the swing rides at the fairs.

But when the happiness of Michaelmas is gone, autumn with its noise of water comes knocking at every door.

Knock, knock.
Who's there?
Autumn again.
What do you want?
The coolness of your temple.
You can't have it.
Then I'll take it.
Knock, knock.
Who's there?
Autumn again.

With the first rain, the threshing floors fill with grass.
The air is a bit chilly now, and no one goes to the park.
Look-at-the-Sky is sitting at his table, his legs tucked
cozily under the green felt tablecloth, his feet warmed
by a charcoal brazier. But the sunsets fill the entire
sky. Enormous clouds annul the landscape and strange
lights go skittering over the rooftops or fall asleep in
the cathedral tower. And here again is the voice of true
melancholy.

> Through that window
> over the river
> toss me your kerchief,
> for I am hurt.

> Through that window
> over the garden
> toss me your kerchief,
> for I am dying.

Through that window
over the water
toss me your kerchief,
I'm nearly dead.

It happens that the boys do not want to go to school:
they are playing with their tops.

It happens that in drawing rooms they are lighting
candles for the deceased.

It happens that we are in November.

It smells like burnt straw, and the piles of leaves (do
you remember?) are beginning to rot. It is raining, and
people are indoors.

But in the middle of the Puerta Real there are already a
few stalls selling noisemakers.

A girl from Armilla or Santa Fe or Atarfe, a year older,
dressed perhaps in mourning, is singing for her master's
children:

Of the four muleteers
who go to the water,
the one with the grey mule
steals my heart.

Of the four muleteers
who go to the river,
the one with the grey mule
is my husband.

We have gone round the year. It will always be like this.
Before and now. We must leave, but Granada remains.
Eternal in time but fleeting in these poor hands — these
hands of mine, the smallest of her children.

Notes

OC refers to volume and page number of Federico García Lorca, *Obras Completas*, ed. Miguel García-Posada (Barcelona: Círculo de Lectores, 1997).

Poem of the Fair (p. 13)

In July 1921, shortly after his twenty-third birthday, Lorca returned to his family's house in the village of Asquerosa, away from the heat and fumes of Madrid, where he had been studying at the Residencia de Estudiantes. A few days after his arrival he wrote to a friend: "I think my place is here, in the midst of these musical poplars and the continuous backwaters of these lyrical rivers. For here my heart is definitively at rest and I can poke fun at my passions, which are always waiting for me, in the tower of the city, like a band of panthers."

In July and August, during his stay in Asquerosa, a few country miles by train and carriage from Granada, he settled down to work on his *Suites*: loosely structured sequences of short poems. The title, *Suites*, is drawn from the world of music, and the structural ideas and whimsical tone seem reminiscent of one of Lorca's favorite composers, Claude Debussy. The idea was to capture some phenomenon – the moon, the hours of evening, the ocean, wheatfields, flamenco – in a series of stylized *estampas* (prints) or "moments." Lorca's first book of verse, *Libro de poemas*, arrived that July from Madrid, but by the time the first copy reached his hands he had grown tired of its sometimes ponderous rhetoric – "path of the essay, path of declamation" – and was struck by the possibilities of the short poem. At the Residencia he had become interested both in haiku and in the lyrics of Andalusian folksong: a fine example of lyrical concentration "for those of us who must prune and care for the over-luxuriant lyrical tree left to us by Romanticism."

Gracefully, with a touch of irony, the *Suites* capture a range of lyrical events and metaphysical conundrums (the longing for childhood, the mystery of language, or the anguish of unrealized possibilities). One of them, dated July 27, 1921, pays homage to the fairs that come to Spanish villages on saints' days in summer and autumn.

This little sheaf of poems, *Poema de la feria*, was tucked away with other *Suites* awaiting revision, and, except for two poems, remained unknown for more than 60 years. In 1931, Lorca had given the MS. to the French Hispanist Mathilde Pomès. Sold at auction after her death, it was bought by the Barcelona bookseller and bibliophile Ramón Soley who published it in facsimile in spring 1997. It is presented here in English for the first time. I have translated from Soley's edition, but have also consulted an unpublished critical edition of the *Suites* by Melissa Dinverno of the University of Michigan.

p. 22   In "Dark Song," Lorca drew a box around lines 12–15, as though considering them for omission.

p. 26   In the final lines of "Variation," Lorca is remembering the traditional Spanish ballad, often sung by children, "Mambrú se fue a la guerra…". Spanish text, *Ferias* (Barcelona: Edicions Delstre, 1997).

Summer Hours (p. 29)
Written August 11, 1921. Complete manuscript published for the first time by C. de Paepe in *Boletín de la Fundación Federico García Lorca*, and given here in English for the first time. Spanish text: *Boletín de la Fundación Federico García Lorca*, no. 16 (December 1994), 16–19.

Palimpsests (p. 37)
Probably written in spring 1922, and published in 1936 in *Primeras canciones*, without "Air" and "Madrigal." The "Vermilion Towers" (*Torres Bermejas*) form part of a wall near the Alhambra. The libidinous Melisendra is the protagonist of a well-known traditional ballad. Spanish text: *OC*, I: 184–186.

Little Tales of the Wind (p. 45)
Written in Asquerosa in July 1922. Spanish text: *OC*, I: 211–213.

Water Jets (p. 51)
Composed 1921–1922. One page of the manuscript is missing.
Lorca published the first poem in *Songs* (1927), entitling it "Granada y 1850." Spanish text: *OC*, I: 266–267.

Meditations and Allegories of the Water (p. 57)
Written, like the preceding letter, in spring 1922, according to Dinverno, but never finished. The Vega is the green, fertile plain at the foot of the Sierra Nevada, where Lorca's father, Federico García Rodríguez, a rich landowner, cultivated sugar beets and other crops. The "border" or "dividing line" mentioned by Lorca lies to the west of the Cubillas, the river mentioned in the opening paragraph. See Ian Gibson, *Lorca's Granada. A Practical Guide* (London: Faber and Faber, 1992), p. 146. Spanish text: *OC*, I: 294–296.

Daydreams of a River (p. 60)
"Ensueños del río" is from the same period as "Meditations…". Both were published in *Collected Poems*, ed. C. Maurer (New York: Farrar, Straus and Giroux, 1990), pp. 324–327 and 318–321.

Granada: Paradise Closed to Many (p. 63)
Published in the catalogue of the Seville Exposition of 1929, and given here for the first time in English, following the text in C. Maurer, ed., *Conferencias*, vol. 1 (Madrid: Alianza Editorial, 1984), pp. 133–136. Lorca read these lines for the first time in 1926 as part of a lecture on the poet Pedro Soto de Rojas (1584–1658), a friend of Lope de Vega and Góngora. His masterpiece, *Paraíso cerrado para muchos, jardines abiertos para pocos*, describes his house and walled garden in Granada. Spanish text: *OC*, III: 79–83.

August (p. 71)
Written *ca.* 1924 and published in *Songs* (1927). Spanish text: *OC*, I: p. 354.

Evening (p. 72)
From *Songs* (1927). Spanish text: *OC*, I: 368.

Ballad of the Three Rivers (p. 73)
From *Poem of the Deep Song*, written 1921 and published 1931. Spanish text: *OC*, I: 305–306.

Tree, tree / dry and green (p. 75)
Written in 1923 and published in *Songs* (1927). Spanish text: *OC*, I: 370–371.

St. Michael (Granada) (p. 77)

From *The Gypsy Ballads* (1928). Written in August 1926. The poem describes the break of dawn on the feast of St. Michael (Sept. 29), an occasion celebrated in Granada with a pilgrimage to the shrine of San Miguel el Alto on the hill over the gypsy quarter of the Albaicín. Lorca is referring to a peculiar Baroque statue portraying a somewhat effeminate archangel. Ramsden explains: "Behind the altar a glass screen [*glass*] separates the nave from the 'camarín' [*alcove of his tower*] where the statue of St. Michael stands surrounded by four lights [*lantern light*]. The boyish figure of the saint [*ephebe of three thousand nights*] [...] sumptuously attired in female dress [...] and with a fine plume of feathers on his head [*feathers*] is treading, somewhat delicately, on the prostrate figure of a demonic, tailed Satan, his right arm upraised with three arrows in his hand [*pointing to twelve o'clock*], threatening the demon beneath his feet." H. Ramsden, *Lorca's Romancero gitano. Eighteen Commentaries* (Manchester: Manchester University Press, 1988), p. 148. Words in italics, mine. Spanish text: *OC*, I: 427–429.

Sleepwalking Ballad (p. 80)

Lorca said of this ballad (written 1924; published in *The Gypsy Ballads*, 1928) that it was "thought by many to express Granada's longing for the sea and the anguish of a city that cannot hear the waves and seeks them in the play of her underground waters and in the undulous clouds with which she covers her mountains. That is true, but this poem is also something else. It is a pure poetic event, of Andalusian essence, and will always have changing lights, even for me, the man who communicated it. If you ask me why I wrote, 'A thousand crystal tambourines / were wounding the dawn,' I will tell you that I saw them in the hands of angels and trees, but I will not be able to say more; certainly I cannot explain their meaning. And that is the way it should be. By means of poetry a man more rapidly approaches the cutting edge that the philospher and the mathematician turn away from in silence." *Deep Song and Other Prose* (New York: New Directions, 1980), pp. 111–112. The mention of the "passes of Cabra," a mountain pass in Córdoba province, suggests that one of the men is a smuggler, wounded in an encounter with the Civil Guard. Spanish text: *OC*, I: 420–422.

Holy Week in Granada (p. 85)

Broadcast on the radio in Madrid in April 1936, a few months before Lorca was murdered in Granada. He spent Holy Week the year before (April 14–21, 1935) not in Granada but in Seville, at the invitation of Joaquín Romero Murube, keeper of the Alcázar, a story he tells about in an interview: "Murube rented a balcony, just for me, where I could watch [the procession]. The gypsies, who are very fond of me, gave me an intimate Holy Week with the best of their wines and their liturgies. They built an altar on top of ten huge casks of wine, with paper roses and burning candles and the pictures of two bullfighters, Joselito and Sánchez Mejías, and before that altar I read for the first time my *Lament for Ignacio Sánchez Mejías*. After that they danced in bare feet and didn't let even my best friends into the room. The only non-gypsy there was me. And that night I slept at the house of *La Malena* [gypsy dancer] in a huge, lovely white bed that smelled sweetly of apple." Later, he sat in the gardens of the Alcázar, chatting with the gardener and gathering material for his comedy *Doña Rosita, or The Language of the Flowers*. Spanish text: *OC*, III: 271–274.

Casida of One Wounded by Water (p. 91)

From *Divan of the Tamarit*, published posthumously in 1940. The Huerta del Tamarit, from which the book takes its name, was a country house owned by one of Lorca's uncles. With its ghazals and casidas, the "Divan" (collection of verse) was a poetic tribute to Arab-Andalusian poetry. Spanish text: *OC*, I: 600.

Casida of the Boughs (p. 92)

From *Divan of the Tamarit*. In his lecture "Play and Theory of the Duende" (1933), Lorca says of artistic inspiration: "The duende does not come at all unless he sees that death is possible. The duende must know beforehand that he can serenade death's house and rock those branches we all wear: branches that do not have, will never have, any consolation" (*Deep Song*, pp. 49–50.) Spanish text: *OC*, I: 601–602.

Ghazal of the Love Which Hides from Sight (p. 93)

Lines 1–2 are from the lyrics of a flamenco piece, a *tanguillo*: "I want to live in Granada / only to hear / the bell of the Vela / when I go to sleep." In his *Handbook for Travellers in Spain* (1:303), Richard Ford explains that the "*torre de la Vela is* so called, because on this watch-tower hangs a silver-tongued bell, which, struck by the warder at certain times, is the primitive clock that gives notice to irrigators below. It is heard on a still night even at Loja, 30 miles off, and tender and touching are the feelings which the silver sound awakens. This bell is also rung every January 2, the anniversary of the surrender of Granada; on that day the Alhambra is visited by crowds of peasantry. Few maidens pass by without striking the bell, which ensures a husband, and a good one in proportion as the noise made, which it need not be said is continuous and considerable. The fete is altogether most national and picturesque." The crown of vervain (*verbena*) in line 3 would be appropriate for a future husband or wife. The rhyme *verbena / Cartagena* was suggested by a children's song. Spanish text: *OC*, I: 594.

Ghaẓal of the Dead Child (p. 94)
From *Divan of the Tamarit*. Spanish text: *OC*, I: 594–595.

Ghaẓal of the Morning Market Place (p. 95)
The "Gateway of Elvira," once the principal entrance to Granada, leads to the gypsy (formerly Moorish) quarter of the Albaicín. Spanish text: *OC*, I: 644.

How a City Sings from November to November (p. 97)
Lecture given in Buenos Aires, October 16, 1933. "My lectures will be illustrated by music, and I am going to sing," Lorca told a journalist in Buenos Aires in October 1933. "I won't sing very loudly, but yes, I will sing, because I believe I'm the only person who can illustrate – no matter how badly I do so – my comments on the origins of Andalusian music."

Throughout his adolescence – until around 1917 – music seemed far more important to Lorca than literature. In a letter to a friend he says that he "took the Holy Orders of music" long before he began to write poetry. By 1918 he was a fine classical pianist, and was making a collection of "the splendid inner polyphony of the folk music of Granada." This songbook, which was to be titled *Tonadas de la Vega* is one of five works said to be "in preparation" on the last page of his first book of prose, *Impresiones y paisajes*. *Tunes of the Vega* was never published, perhaps never even compiled, though in the 1930s Lorca boasted to the musician Marcelle Schweitzer that he had collected over 300 folksongs from Granada and could play them by heart. He had gathered many of them in the company of his beloved mentor Manuel de Falla, with whom he collaborated on puppet plays, a great festival of *cante jondo*, and an unfinished musical play entitled *La comedianta (The Actress)*.

Lorca's love of folk music inspired several of his lectures, among them the famous defense of *cante jondo*, first given in 1922, revised in 1930 and read "as a polemic" in different cities of Cuba, Argentina and Spain. In January, 1928 he announces to a friend that he is writing a lecture about the pathos of the Spanish cradle song, and when he read it the following December to his friends at the Residencia de Estudiantes, Madrid, he himself sang the lullabies. Federico de Onís, who taught Spanish literature at Columbia University when Lorca studied there in 1929–1930, tells us that "His voice was not an extraordinarily good one for singing; it might almost be called defective; a little hoarse and weak, though when he was speaking or reading aloud it acquired expressiveness and personality."

Like the singers of *cante jondo*, Lorca relied on *duende* – on his own dark personal charm – rather than on polish and style. Whom else could he trust to sing his favorite songs, neither embellishing them nor falsifying their rhythms? "Songs," he said, "are creatures, delicate creatures whose rhythm one must take pains not to alter. Each one is a miracle of equilibrium, like a silver coin on the point of a needle. Songs are like people. They live and perfect themselves. Some degenerate and crumble away until they are nothing but palimpsests, full of lacunae and things that make no sense."

In "folksongs worn down by time" he found poetic mystery, a quality he sought for his own works. "How a City Sings..." is not only an attempt to define the lyrical essence of Granada, or, defeating time and space, to evoke its beauty for others; as in almost all of his lectures, Lorca is revealing the forces that nurtured his own art, and trying to capture the essence of Granada.

First published by Mario Hernández in his edition of Federico García Lorca, *Federico y su mundo*, 2nd ed. (Madrid: Alianza Editorial, 1982), pp. 471–485. Published for the first time in English in this translation in a limited edition (San Francisco: Cadmus Editions, 1982).

p. 97   Wolf notes are known as *gallos* (roosters) in Spanish.

p. 97   In his story "Santa Lucía y San Lázaro" Lorca writes: "St. Lucy was a beautiful maiden of Syracuse. In paintings she is shown holding her two magnificent ox-like eyes on a tray. She suffered martyrdom under the consul Pascasian…". *OC*, I:488. The story of her life is told by Jacobus de Voragine in *The Golden Legend*.

p. 97   *Alfajor, torta alajú, mantecado.* There are no English equivalents for these Spanish pastries, two of which are mentioned in Lorca's 1928 lecture on Spanish cradle songs: "To know the Alhambra of Granada…, before touring its rooms and courtyards, it is very useful, of great pedagogical value, to sample the delicious *alfajor* of Zafra or the *tortas alajú* made by the nuns. The taste and fragrance of these sweets give us the authentic temperature of the palace when it was alive – the ancient light, the cardinal points of its courtly temperament." *Deep Song*, p. 8.

p. 98   *Songs that cannot fly.* In the earlier lecture on lullabies, Lorca had distinguished between folksongs that stray from their native regions to other parts of Spain, e.g., the *bolero*, and songs which do not. See *Deep Song*, p. 22.

p. 99   *"What pain and what despair…".* Titled "Generalife" and dedicated by the great Spanish poet Juan Ramón Jiménez to Lorca's sister Isabel. Isabel and Federico had accompanied Jiménez to the Alhambra when he visited Granada in summer 1924.

p. 100   *The prose of Bécquer.* Gustavo Adolfo Bécquer (1836–1870), Spain's greatest Romantic lyric poet.

p. 100   In his youth Lorca witnessed a revival of Renaissance Spanish music for the *vihuela*, including that of Luis de Narvaez, a native of Granada (1530–1550), who published a collection of pieces for that instrument.

p. 100   *Debussy.* In his lecture on *cante jondo* (1922), Lorca writes that in Debussy's "Vague, tender *Soirée en Grenade*… one can find all the emotional themes of the night in Granada: the blue remoteness of the Vega, the Sierra greeting the tremulous Mediterranean, the enormous barbs of the clouds which sink into the distance, the admirable rubato of the city, the hallucinating play of its underground waters." *Deep Song*, pp. 29–30.

p. 101   *Don Pedro* is the protagonist of Calderón's *The Surgeon of*

His Honor and the subject of Lorca's "Romance con lagunas" (Ballad with Lagoons) in *The Gypsy Ballads*. Don Alonso is the hero of Lope de Vega's *El caballero de Olmedo*. Duke Octavio of Naples is one of the characters in Tirso de Molina's play about Don Juan. *Miguel de Mañara*, the seventeenth-century Spanish sinner and mystic, has often been compared to Don Juan.

p. 101   The *zambomba* is a sort of friction drum used in Christmas festivities: its membrane is pierced with a stick which the player moves up and down.

p. 101   "The Four Muleteers" was one of the songs Lorca recorded with *La Argentinita* in 1931 (now available on CD from Sonifolk, Madrid). He told a journalist in Buenos Aires, "it is the typical Christmas carol of the Albaicín. It is only sung at Christmas, when the weather is cold. It is a pagan carol, like almost all of the ones sung by the people. The religious carols are only sung in the churches and to put children to sleep. It is very strange, this pagan carol, which reveals Andalusia's Bacchic sense of the Nativity" (*OC*, III: 484).

p. 102   *From Granada to Africa*. The musicologist Theodore Grame writes that this *músiquí andalusí*, which still flourishes in Northern Africa, "was originally the court music of Muslim Andalusia and was carried from there to North Africa by the many intellectuals, artisans and musicians who fled after the fall of the Kingdom of Granada in 1492." See *The New Grove Dictionary of Music and Musicians*, ed. Stanley Sadie, vol. 12 (London: Macmillan, 1980), p. 588.

p. 102   *Tambourines and chicharras*. The *pandereta* is a tambourine with jingles, and the *chicharra* a tube, one end of which is covered with a parchment membrane pierced by a piece of waxed thread. When the thread is moved it makes a cricket-like sound. *Carrañacas*: Two notched pieces of wood rubbed together. The "copper mortars" are turned upside down and played like bells.

p. 102   *Joyous Christmas ballad*. One of the songs recorded by Lorca with *La Argentinita*. Lorca remarks in an interview in Buenos Aires that he knew two versions of this song: "One has a gay rhythm and is sung in the Vega; the other is melancholy and comes from the Sierra" (*OC*, III: 483).

p. 105   *Uyuí*. The word is illegible in the manuscript; perhaps *uyuiy*. Lorca seems to be referring to the stylized shout of joy that ends certain folksongs.

p. 106 *San Nicolás*. A square in the northern part of Granada commanding a view of the Alhambra and the Sierra Nevada.

p. 106 *I come from the poplars, mother...* Lines 5–6, on Granada, do not appear in the version of this song found in Juan Vázquez's *Recopilación de sonetos y villancicos a cuatro y cinco voces* (Seville, 1560). Did Lorca invent them? *Miguel de Fuenllana* and *Diego Pisador* are sixteenth-century composers of *vihuela* music. *Juan del Encina* is remembered for his plays, and *Francisco de Salinas* for his theoretical work on music, *De musica libri septem*.

p. 108 *Comadre* is the form of address used by two women from the same village.

p. 108 *The church bells of San Juan de Dios*. In this church, dedicated in 1759, is a reredos of gilded wood "of such singular style that the most delirious imagination would, today, be quite incapable of conceiving it". Manuel Gómez Moreno, *Guía de Granada*, 1892, p. 358.

p. 109 *Elvira Street*. The poet's brother tells us that this is a local folksong, a *fandanguillo* (*Federico y su mundo*, p. 364). The *manolas* – women dressed in typical costume – are mentioned in "St. Michael" and brought to life in the last act of Lorca's play *Doña Rosita*.

p. 109 *The last firecracker*. On p. 17 of the manuscript Lorca crossed out the following words: "Last summer I had gotten together with some friends, popular types, who were singing. A firecracker went off nearby and no one was the least bit perturbed. One of them simply said: 'That was just a clap that came in at the wrong time.'"

p. 109 *Under the leaf...* Another of the songs recorded by Lorca and *La Argentinita*.

p. 112 *St. Michael*. See above, p. 77. The "sea of fruits" mentioned in the next paragraph refers to those sold at the stands set up on Michaelmas in the vicinity of the shrine.

p. 113 *Knock, knock...* Lorca's poem imitates traditional children's rhymes.

p. 114 *Candles for the deceased*, on All Souls Day, November 2.

EL CAFE DE CHINITAS

Recogída y armonízada por Federico García Lorca

Allegro moderato

En el Ca- fé de Chi- ni tas dí- jo

Pa- quí ro a su her-ma no en el Ca- fé de Chi-

ni- tas dí jo Pa- quí ro a su her-ma no Soy más va-

lien te que tú más to- re- ro y más gí-

(El Café de Chínitas)

ta - no, soy más va - lien - te que tú más to -

re - ro y más gi - ta - no.

LAS TRES HOJAS

Recogida y armonizada por Federico García Lorca

De ba - jo de la ho - ja de la ver,
ten - go a mi a - man - te ma - lo, Je - sús qué

be - na
pe - na
de - ba,
de - ba - jo, de - ba - jo, de la

ho - ja
de - ba - jo, de - ba - jo, de la ho - ja

de - ba - jo de la ho - ja de la ver - be - na.